ELVIS
Presley
The
KING

Katherine E. Krohn

Lerner Publications Company ▪ Minneapolis

*This book is dedicated to my
music-loving family in Tennessee.*

This book is available in two bindings:
Library binding by Lerner Publications Company
Soft cover by First Avenue Editions
241 First Avenue North
Minneapolis, MN 55401

LIBRARY OF CONGRESS CATALOGING-IN-PUBLICATION DATA

Krohn, Katherine E.
Elvis Presley: the king / Katherine E. Krohn.
p. cm—(The Achievers)
Intended audience: Grades 4-9.
Summary: Examines the childhood, musical career, films,
family life, and legacy of the rock star Elvis Presley.
ISBN 0-8225-2877-0 (library binding)
ISBN 0-8225-9654-7 (paperback)
1. Presley, Elvis, 1935-1977—Juvenile literature. 2 Rock
musicians—United States—Bibliography—Juvenile literature.
[1. Presley, Elvis, 1935-1977. 2. Singers. 3. Rock music.]
I. Title. II. Series.
ML3930.P73K76   1993
782.42166'092—dc20   93-23905
[B]   CIP
                                                MN AC

Manufactured in the United States of America

1 2 3 4 5 6 – I/JR – 99 98 97 96 95 94

Contents

Elvis Presley would turn the music world upside down.

1

Shake, Rattle, and Roll

"Ladies and Gentlemen, we have a *really big show* tonight!" said TV variety-show host Ed Sullivan. "Here is Elvis Presley!"

The man who walked onstage that night in January 1957 hardly needed an introduction. A year earlier, Elvis Presley had entered the American music scene like a steam locomotive. People everywhere were talking about Elvis.

Elvis took a few hard swipes at his guitar. He shook his shoulders. "I'm ready to rock and roll," he sang. The crowd went crazy. Boys stomped their feet and clapped their hands. Girls screamed and pulled their hair. Elvis swiveled his hips and the girls yelled louder.

Although the studio audience was enjoying Elvis's lively performance, the show's producers were worried. Concerned that television viewers might be offended by the act, producers insisted that Elvis be filmed from the waist up—so his swirling hips and jumpy legs wouldn't appear on screen. Despite this censorship, Elvis did what he could to keep his act alive. He tossed his head more and shook his shoulders harder.

At first Ed Sullivan hadn't wanted Elvis Presley as a guest on his popular program. Some people, especially parents, didn't like the new "rock and roll" music that Elvis sang. And they didn't like Elvis—with his jet black hair, good looks, daring costumes, and wild concerts.

Across the United States, schoolteachers and religious leaders protested Elvis's "torso-tossing" performances. Some journalists called his act obscene. Elvis tried to defend himself. "When I sing, I just start jumping," he told a reporter. "I just act the way I feel."

Finally, mostly to boost his show's ratings, Ed Sullivan invited Elvis to perform on his program. Sullivan paid the 22-year-old singer more money than any guest had ever received—$50,000 for three appearances.

After meeting Elvis, Sullivan formed a new opinion of the star. Elvis called Sullivan "Sir," and he always said "thank you" to his applauding fans. His manners surprised and impressed Sullivan. Even though Elvis was a celebrity, he never acted rude or demanding. "I want to say to Elvis Presley and the country," Sullivan announced to 54 million television viewers at the end of the third show, "this is a real, decent, fine boy."

Teenagers went wild for Elvis.

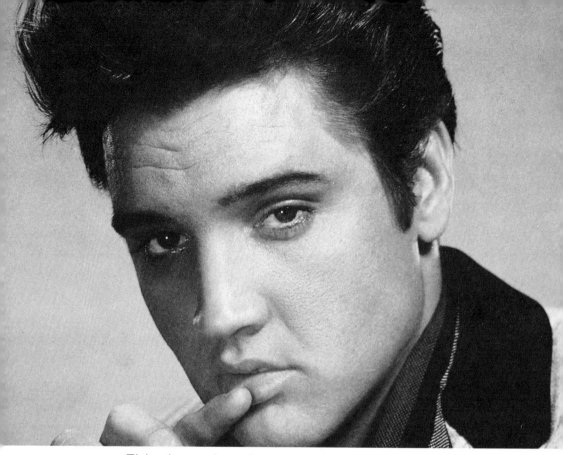

Elvis charmed moviegoers and music fans alike.

Sullivan's speech helped change Elvis's reputation. The critics soon calmed down. Those people
who hated Elvis learned to tolerate him. His fans,
of course, only loved him more. Some went to great
extremes to see their hero. Young people waited
for hours outside Elvis's house in Memphis, Tennessee. "I stood by the gate when there wasn't
another soul around," reported one teen. "I sat in
the rain. I got pneumonia." Other fans stole water

from Elvis's swimming pool and plucked blades of grass from his lawn.

Elvis was from the South. He first started singing at church. He attended all-night gospel shows and sang religious songs called spirituals. "Some of those spirituals had big, heavy rhythm beats like a rock and roll song," he remembered. "That music didn't hurt anybody, and it sure made you feel good." Country music also influenced Elvis, as did rhythm and blues (R&B), the African-American folk music he heard on the streets near his home in Memphis.

Elvis Presley recorded his first hit single, "Heartbreak Hotel," in January 1956. Music fans couldn't get enough of his deep, soulful voice or the song's rock and roll beat. The record sold more than a million copies. Later that year, Elvis starred in his first Hollywood film, *Love Me Tender*. This time, audiences enjoyed not only Elvis's singing talent but also his bewitching brown eyes and his crooked smile. The title song, a ballad, became another best-selling single.

Before long Elvis was a millionaire. He had been very poor as a child, and he enjoyed his new wealth. He bought flashy clothes, cars, and jewelry. Blue suede shoes became his trademark. Elvis even went through a "pink phase" for a while—he wore pink suits and drove a pink Cadillac.

Elvis soon became so famous that people around the globe knew him by his first name alone. He could hardly believe his rapid rise to success. "I don't know what it is," he laughed. "But I sure hope it doesn't stop."

Everyone wanted Elvis's autograph.

2

Lot o' Livin' to Do

Elvis Aaron Presley was born on January 8, 1935, in Tupelo, Mississippi. His parents were Gladys Love and Vernon Elvis Presley. Elvis had an identical twin brother, Jesse Garon, who died at birth.

Elvis grew up during the Great Depression, an economic crisis that affected nearly everyone in the United States. Many people lost their jobs. Others lost their businesses or homes. The depression hit small towns like Tupelo especially hard.

Vernon and Gladys Presley worked odd jobs to make a living. Vernon hoed cotton, picked corn, and drove a truck for a dairy. Gladys worked at the Tupelo Garment Company as a sewing machine operator. She worked twelve hours a day, six days a week. "My mother took in extra washing and sewing to see us through," Elvis remembered.

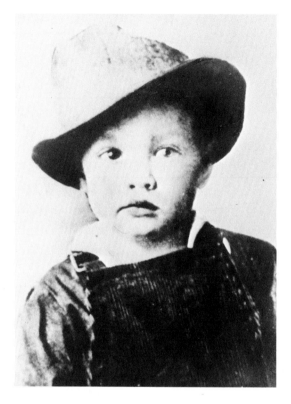
Little Elvis, age 3

The Presleys rented a simple, two-room house with a swing on the front porch. The house didn't have indoor plumbing—water for drinking and bathing had to be carried to the house from a well in the yard.

Elvis didn't have brothers or sisters and he had few friends. "I felt like I didn't fit in," he said. After school Elvis sometimes visited his grandmother, Minnie Mae Presley, who lived next door.

"All I looked forward to was Sunday," Elvis said, "when we all could go to church." There, at the First Assembly of God on Adams Street, Elvis could do what he loved best—sing.

When Elvis was 10 years old, he entered a talent contest at the Mississippi-Alabama Fair and Dairy Show. Standing on a chair in front of a crowd of strangers, he sang "Old Shep," a sad song about a dying dog. The audience and the judges liked his performance. Elvis was thrilled to win second prize—free admission to the amusement rides and a five-dollar bill.

Vernon and Gladys gave Elvis a guitar for his 11th birthday. At first he was disappointed with the gift—he had asked for a bicycle. But he soon grew to appreciate the guitar. He taught himself a few simple chords and sang along, copying the musicians he heard on the radio. Elvis liked the "Grand Ole Opry," a live radio show broadcast every Saturday night from Nashville, Tennessee. He especially enjoyed the cowboy singers.

In 1948 Vernon and Gladys decided to move to Memphis. Vernon had lost a truck-driving job, and the Presleys could barely pay their bills. They knew they would find more opportunities in a larger city. "We packed everything we could into our old Plymouth and moved on," Gladys recalled. "Things just had to get better."

The Presleys never dreamed their son would become a star.

The Presleys moved into a run-down, one-bedroom apartment. Elvis slept on the couch. Minnie Mae, who had also come to Memphis, slept on a cot in the living room. Vernon found a good job almost immediately, driving a delivery truck for a paint company. Gladys took a part-time sewing job.

Elvis, now 13, entered high school. L. C. Humes High in Memphis was three times the size of his former school. At first Elvis had trouble making friends. He was shy and he looked different from the other kids. He wore stylish clothes and a "ducktail" haircut. "I liked my hair long because that was the way the truck drivers wore it," Elvis explained.

In the early 1950s, many teenagers attended "hops" and "bops"—fun dance parties featuring the latest hits by singers like Frank Sinatra and Doris Day. After school, teens hung out in soda shops and slipped nickels into jukeboxes. They listened to syrupy love songs with lush instrumental backups.

But Elvis was different. In *his* spare time, he liked to roam a neighborhood called "Shake Rag." There, he heard street musicians play rhythm and blues. Many African Americans expressed their struggles and stories through R&B music. The hard-driving rhythms and simple lyrics impressed Elvis. He had never heard street musicians before. Nor had he heard music played with such emotion. "I realized then that music—the blues, gospel, or whatever—is all about letting out what you're feeling inside," said Elvis.

Throughout high school, Elvis took auto shop classes, preparing himself for a career as a mechanic. He received passing grades in most subjects, but, surprisingly, he failed the first semester of his music class. Music theory meant little to Elvis—he just liked to sing.

One day the music class held a talent show, and Elvis performed before his teacher and classmates. He was nervous and afraid the other kids would laugh at him. Accompanying himself on guitar, Elvis sang an R&B number called "Long Black Train."

The students sat in silence while Elvis performed. Most of them had never heard a rhythm and blues song before, and they hadn't heard *anyone* sing like Elvis. The music seemed to come from someplace deep inside him. The students didn't laugh at Elvis. Instead they cheered.

"Everything seemed to change for me that day," Elvis said. "After that I could always count on my music to help me make friends—especially girls."

Soon Elvis started dating. He joined the school football team and took a part-time job as an usher at Loew's State Theater. Elvis liked expensive clothes. To pay for his growing wardrobe, he took a second part-time job, as a shop assistant at Marl Metal Products Company.

In 1952 the Presleys moved to Lauderdale Courts, a housing project in Memphis for low-income families. There, Elvis made friends with Regis Wilson, a classmate at Humes High. They dated for a few months, and in June 1953, Elvis took Regis to the senior prom. Regis wore a fluffy pink gown. Elvis wore a dark suit and blue suede shoes. "Elvis told me he didn't know how to dance," Regis recalled. "So we sat and talked and drank Cokes all night."

After graduation, Elvis worked for a short time in a factory. Then he took a job driving a truck for the Crown Electric Company. He was pleased with his pay—$1.25 an hour.

In August 1953, Elvis decided to give his mother a unique birthday gift. He saw an advertisement for the Memphis Recording Studio: "WE RECORD ANYTHING - ANYTIME - ANYWHERE, $2 One Side, $4 Two Sides." Gladys Presley loved to hear Elvis sing. He would make his mother a record.

Assistant technician Marion Keisker greeted Elvis when he came to the recording studio. Curious, she looked Elvis up and down. With his well-groomed hair and fancy clothes, he didn't look like a typical customer.

Most amateur singers imitated the famous musicians they heard on the radio. They tried to sing like Frank Sinatra or Hank Williams. "Who do you sound like?" Keisker asked Elvis.

"I don't sound like nobody," Elvis replied.

He handed Keisker four dollars and recorded two of his favorite songs—"My Happiness," made famous by the Inkspots, and a country ballad, "That's When Your Heartaches Begin." Elvis hated the result. "[The record] sounded like someone beating on a bucket lid," he said.

But Keisker had a different opinion. While Elvis sang, she recorded a second tape. She wanted her boss, Sam Phillips, to hear the record. Phillips operated Sun Records out of the same studio.

"I heard in Elvis...what I guess they now call 'soul,'" Keisker remembered. "So I taped it. I wanted Sam to know." She asked Elvis for his phone number—just in case.

Sam Phillips liked the Presley tape. But he liked a lot of other singers too. He told Keisker to file the recording away. For weeks Elvis waited for a call from the studio. He gave up hope after a while.

Months later Phillips heard a demonstration, or "demo," tape of a ballad called "Without You." The beautiful and haunting lyrics, performed by an unknown studio singer, impressed Phillips. He wanted to record the song—but he needed the right vocalist. Keisker reminded him about Elvis Presley—"the kid with the interesting voice." *He* could sing ballads.

Phillips gave Elvis a call. "[I had] barely been able to hang up the telephone," Phillips recalled, "before Elvis came bursting through the door, eager to start."

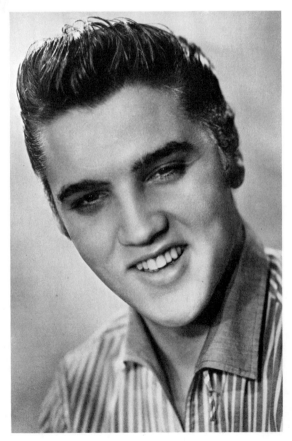

Most young men wore crew cuts in the 1950s. But Elvis liked to grow his hair long on top.

3

Elvis the Pelvis

"Kid, you have to do better than *this*," Sam Phillips said, shaking his head. "Let's take a coffee break." As soon as Phillips left the room, Elvis pounded the wall with his fists. His big chance to cut a song at Sun Records had arrived—and he was blowing it!

He had listened carefully to the demo tape of "Without You." He sang the ballad exactly as it sounded on the demo. But no matter how hard Elvis tried, Phillips told him to sing the song again. His throat hurt and he could hardly think straight. His backup musicians, Bill Black and Scotty Moore, were getting restless.

To break the tension, Elvis grabbed a guitar. He started singing one of his favorite blues songs, "That's All Right, Mama." Instead of strumming the strings, Elvis banged on the guitar like a drum. The studio musicians joined in with enthusiasm.

Phillips froze in his steps as he reentered the studio. The hair on the back of his neck stood on end. "The sound I heard was electric!" Phillips said. At that moment, he knew he had discovered something important—Elvis Presley singing like Elvis Presley, not like someone else. Phillips wasted no time. He asked Elvis to sing the song again. This time Phillips recorded it.

On Monday, July 5, 1954, Elvis finished making his first record. The disc (called a "45") featured "That's All Right, Mama," with "Blue Moon of Kentucky," a country song, on the flip side.

Two days later, Dewey Phillips spun the 45 on his popular "Red Hot and Blue" radio show on WHBQ in Memphis. While listeners heard "That's All Right, Mama" for the first time, Elvis hid in a movie theater. He was afraid people would laugh at him.

That night the phone at WHBQ rang off the hook. People wanted to hear the song again. They wanted to know all about Elvis Presley. Why hadn't they heard him before? Where could they buy his record?

A few listeners called the station to complain. They insisted that Elvis must be a black man because he sang rhythm and blues. During the 1950s, most radio stations—which were owned by whites—wouldn't play traditional black music like rhythm and blues. But by performing his own version of rock and roll—greatly inspired by African-American music—Elvis united black and white styles. The results were powerful.

By the end of July, "That's All Right, Mama" had seized the number-three spot on the Memphis record charts. Elvis was amazed by his sudden popularity. Calling themselves "the Blue Moon Boys," Elvis, Bill, and Scotty began singing in nightclubs around Memphis. Elvis's life was changing quickly.

Bill, Elvis, and Scotty

Few people outside Memphis heard Elvis's music, though. Sam Phillips knew that Elvis needed to move ahead fast—while he was hot. Phillips phoned a friend at Nashville's "Grand Ole Opry." Did the radio producers want a fresh new act? They did. Without hesitation, Elvis quit his job at Crown Electric, packed his bags, and headed to Nashville with Scotty and Bill.

Elvis stood on the Opry stage at the Ryman Auditorium and sang "That's All Right, Mama" to a full house. He could hardly believe his good luck. Thousands of people across the country were listening—their radios tuned to WSM, Nashville. Since childhood, Elvis had dreamed of singing on the legendary show.

But when Elvis finished his song, the audience hardly clapped. Some people even booed! Trembling, Elvis walked backstage. Opry manager Jim Denny took him aside. "We don't play that kind of music around here," Denny said. "I think you'd better go back to driving trucks." Apparently, Elvis wasn't "country-music enough" for the Opry crowd.

Devastated, Elvis returned to Memphis. He refused to appear in public for weeks. Finally, in October 1954, Phillips coaxed Elvis back to work. He arranged for Elvis to perform on another nationally broadcast radio program, "The Louisiana Hayride," from KWKH in Shreveport.

Elvis at the Hayride

Elvis and the band piled into Scotty's Chevy. Elvis was worried. What if he bombed on the Hayride like he had at the Opry? Elvis knew this second chance at stardom might be his last.

Fortunately, Shreveport was ready for Elvis Presley. The Hayride audience loved his act! In fact, he caused such a sensation that the producers asked Elvis to return the following week. Soon Elvis signed a one-year contract with the show.

Meanwhile, Elvis steadily put out records. Music critics applauded his second release, another R&B tune, "Good Rockin' Tonight." In January 1955, Elvis produced his third Sun Records single, "Milkcow Blues Boogie." Elvis and the band put on concerts as far away as New Mexico to promote the new records. "Everywhere we went, the crowds got bigger and the girls got wilder," he recalled.

In May Elvis launched his first major concert tour. Country star Hank Snow headlined the three-week engagement, which also featured Mother Maybelle and the Carter Sisters, Slim Whitman, and Faron Young—all Nashville favorites.

Hank Snow's manager, Colonel Thomas A. Parker, approached Elvis after a show. "Son," Parker said, putting his hand on Elvis's shoulder, "you need good management. Let me take over from here." Colonel Parker had a reputation for being persuasive and smart. Without delay Elvis signed on with the Colonel's management agency, All Star Attractions.

The Colonel wasted no time. He knew that Sun Records, a small studio, could take Elvis only so far. Parker wanted Elvis to work for a major record company. For weeks he negotiated with top executives in the recording business. In November 1955, Elvis signed with RCA Records.

Two days after his 21st birthday, on January 10, 1956, Elvis recorded his first single at RCA, "Heartbreak Hotel." The 45 was released two weeks later, and within a month, it landed in *Billboard* magazine's "Top Forty" list of hits.

Colonel Parker gives Elvis some advice.

Elvis's swirling hips shocked many Americans.

Elvis was elated. As his first hit sizzled in the charts and sold like mad, thousands of dollars poured into his bank account. Elvis had never seen so much money! He bought his parents a new house. He bought himself a shiny, black Cadillac.

In June Elvis made his first television appearance, on "The Milton Berle Show." As he sang his hot new release, "Hound Dog," his hips twitched and his shoulders shivered. He tossed his head and sneered a little. The people in the audience lost control. They screamed and clapped.

Newspapers and magazines nationwide carried word of Elvis's TV debut. "Spasms ran through both his legs, and soon the entire midsection of his body was jolting as if he'd swallowed a jackhammer," wrote C. Robert Jennings in the *Saturday Evening Post*. Another reporter nicknamed him "Elvis the Pelvis." A critic from the *New York Herald Tribune* called Elvis "unspeakably untalented and vulgar."

But the same dance moves that some people found offensive caused others to squeal with delight. Elvis was puzzled by all the commotion. "The first time I appeared onstage, it scared me to death," Elvis recalled. "I didn't know what the yelling was about. I didn't realize my body was moving!"

4

Flip, Flop, and Fly

Luckily, Elvis had far more fans than critics. Teenagers felt especially strong about their new idol. "He just feels the rhythm," one boy said. "He digs it the most."

"He isn't afraid to express himself," a 15-year-old girl told *Life* magazine in August 1956. "When he does that on TV, I get down on the floor and scream."

Fan mail, more than 3,000 letters a week, poured into the Presley home. New Elvis records, such as "Don't Be Cruel," "Flip, Flop, and Fly," and "Blue Suede Shoes," climbed the charts. Elvis souvenirs sold in stores across the United States. Fans could buy Elvis jeans, T-shirts, bobby socks, wallets, address books, and charm bracelets. They could take home a glow-in-the-dark photo of Elvis or a tube of Elvis Presley Lipstick—in "Heartbreak Hotel Pink" or "Hound Dog Orange."

As his fame grew, so did his wealth. Elvis purchased a stately Memphis mansion, which he called "Graceland." Vernon, Gladys, and Grandma Minnie Mae moved to Graceland with him. He bought a purple Lincoln Continental and three more Cadillacs. "If I ever go broke," Elvis joked, "I can always open a used car lot!"

Although Elvis enjoyed his singing success, he wanted more. "I want to be a dramatic actor," he told *Newsweek* magazine. The word spread fast. By the fall of 1956, Elvis had snared his first screen role, in the Twentieth Century Fox film *Love Me Tender*. Elvis played the part of a nice southern boy who loses in love and dies tragically.

Some critics raved about Elvis's screen debut. "Nobody in the audience howled or shrieked or moaned or went out of their mind or anything," wrote Janet Winn of the *New Republic*, "because they realized that Elvis is a real actor."

But most reviewers made fun of Elvis's performance. They said he couldn't act. Elvis was bothered by the mixed reviews at first. But later he shrugged and said, "That's the way the mop flops."

Top: Elvis was close to his parents, Vernon and Gladys.
Bottom: Graceland—the King's castle

Despite criticism, *Love Me Tender* was a huge box-office success—earning six times as much money as it cost to produce. Hollywood *wanted* Elvis. His name, good looks, and personality drew people to the theaters.

In July 1957, Elvis made his second film appearance, in Paramount Pictures' *Loving You*. By the end of the year, MGM Studios had released *Jailhouse Rock*. In this movie, Elvis played Vince Everett, a nice guy who accidentally kills a man in a barroom brawl. Vince takes up singing in prison and eventually becomes a star.

In one scene, Elvis sang the hit song "Jailhouse Rock." Costumed in a striped T-shirt and a black suit, he performed a difficult dance routine with several other men dressed as prisoners. Elvis later said the memorable scene was his favorite song-and-dance number.

After Paramount produced Elvis's fourth film, *King Creole*, in the spring of 1958, the United States armed forces called Elvis for a different kind of role. He was drafted into the army.

Assigned to Bad Nauheim, an army base in West Germany, Elvis requested no star treatment, special favors, or extra attention. He wanted to be treated like any other soldier. He would work on the base driving a jeep, and he refused to entertain at army functions.

Sergeant Presley couldn't avoid the cameras.

Before shipping out to Germany, Elvis received terrible news. His mother had suffered a fatal heart attack in Memphis. She was 42. Elvis felt like his world had ended. First his career had been stopped in its tracks by his military service. Then his mother had passed away. "Everything I have is gone," Elvis cried at the funeral. Halfheartedly, he returned to his army duties.

After nearly two years in the army, Elvis was promoted to sergeant. He bought a simple, white-brick house near the base. Vernon and Minnie Mae came to Germany to live with him.

In late 1959, Elvis was discharged from the army. He would return to the United States in a few months. Elvis looked forward to leaving Germany—he missed Tennessee and he yearned to make music again. Elvis didn't know that something very special was about to happen.

To celebrate his upcoming departure, Elvis threw a party and invited a few close friends to his home. One friend brought along a new acquaintance, an air force colonel's daughter named Priscilla Beaulieu. Priscilla, only 14, was smart and shy. She had long brown hair and brilliant blue eyes.

"You're the first girl I've met from the States in a long time," Elvis told Priscilla. He wanted to know about the music scene back home. "Who are the kids listening to?" he asked the young girl.

"Are you kidding?" Priscilla laughed. "Everyone listens to you."

Elvis liked Priscilla instantly. Priscilla liked him too. But she couldn't believe that someone as famous as Elvis Presley was interested in her. Over the next few weeks, Elvis and Priscilla saw as much of each other as possible. But soon, on March 1, 1960, Elvis boarded a plane for the United

States. "As he waved goodbye," Priscilla recalled, "I wondered if I'd ever see him again."

Fighting back tears, Elvis took a long look at Priscilla Beaulieu. Without a doubt, he knew that she was the girl he wanted to marry.

Priscilla Beaulieu was just 14 when she first met Elvis.

5

Falling Star

When his plane landed at Fort Dix, New Jersey, Elvis wasn't sure what to expect. He hadn't performed for two years. Had his fans forgotten him?

Then Elvis saw the crowd waiting at the airport. Hundreds of smiling faces were there to greet him! Loyal fans held "We Love You" and "Welcome Home, Elvis" signs high in the air. As he exited the plane, teenagers screamed and tugged at his clothing. Everyone from schoolchildren to grandmothers begged for autographs.

While Elvis had been in Germany, his fans had doubled in number. They had bought more than five million records.

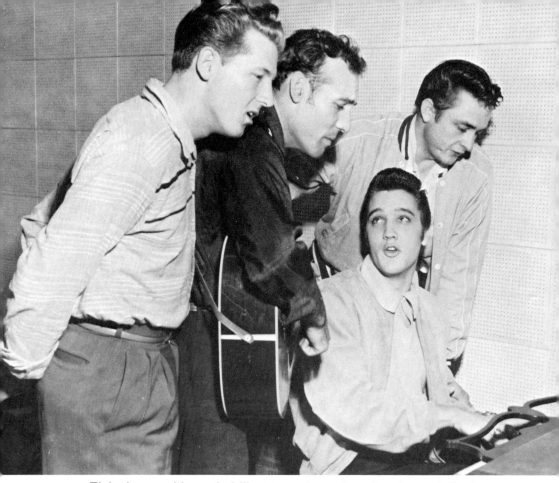

Elvis jams with rockabilly stars Jerry Lee Lewis and Carl Perkins and country legend Johnny Cash.

Colonel Parker hadn't forgotten Elvis either. He quickly put his top recording artist back to work. With his 1960 album, *Elvis Is Back*, Elvis said "hello again" to his faithful fans. The record was an enormous success and reestablished Elvis as the most popular singer in the United States.

Next, Elvis returned to Hollywood. In *G.I. Blues*,

Elvis played an American serviceman with lots of singing talent. Viewers flocked to theaters to see Elvis in a role that somewhat resembled his recent army experience. As new Elvis singles like "Are You Lonesome Tonight?" and "It's Now or Never" sold by the millions, Elvis went to work on another film, Paramount's *Flaming Star*.

By 1963 Elvis's career was again flying high. He was famous, wealthy, and had plenty of admirers. Elvis had no special girlfriend, though, and he often thought of Priscilla Beaulieu. They had exchanged many letters since he left West Germany. He missed her and wanted to see her again. He wondered, did she miss him too?

There was only one way to find out. Elvis called Priscilla in Germany and invited her to visit him at Graceland. Priscilla was thrilled with the invitation—but her parents had mixed feelings. Why did a famous rock star want to date their daughter? Would he break her heart? On the other hand, how could they say no and destroy what could be the opportunity of a lifetime for Priscilla? With some hesitation, the Beaulieus allowed the visit, and Priscilla and Elvis were reunited.

Over the next several months, Priscilla visited Elvis many times. Eventually she moved into Graceland with Elvis and his family. At Graceland 17-year-old Priscilla was treated like a princess.

Viva Las Vegas with Ann-Margret

She rode horses and bought all the clothes she wanted. She enrolled at Immaculate Conception, an all-girls high school in Memphis, and Elvis hired a private tutor to help her with her studies. Vernon and his new wife became her substitute parents. While Elvis was away making films, Priscilla busied herself with school activities.

Over the next few years, Elvis starred in films such as *Blue Hawaii, Roustabout,* and *Harum Scarum.* Most of these movies featured upbeat song-and-dance routines and revolved around a simple plot. Elvis often played a "rough character" who meets a woman, falls in love, and settles down. Almost every Elvis film had a happy ending.

In *Viva Las Vegas*, Elvis played Lucky, a race car driver who comes to Las Vegas for a big race. There, he gets a crush on a beautiful swimming instructor, Rusty, played by Ann-Margret. By the movie's end, Lucky wins the race as well as Rusty's love.

Eventually, Elvis grew tired of making movies. He felt out of place in the fast-paced world of Hollywood. "He's really one of the most sincere people in the most insincere town on earth," commented one actress. Elvis yearned to be in Memphis with Priscilla and his family. But he had signed film contracts years in advance. He was obligated to make movies—two or three a year.

Acting in films like *Girls, Girls, Girls* and *Tickle Me* bothered Elvis. "The scripts were so bad I'd actually get physically ill," he remembered. "I guess I cared too much."

Gradually, Elvis's fame began to work against him. He couldn't go out in public without being swamped by fans. After work, he hid indoors. His loneliness grew. "Boy, I'd have given anything in the world to go get a hamburger with you guys," Elvis told musician friend Bob Moore. "I never had any idea it was going to get like this."

As a musician, Elvis was also frustrated. "I was getting further and further from what was happening in the music scene," he said. "I was cutting sound tracks for movies, while the Beatles, the Rolling Stones, and Bob Dylan were all over the charts."

The months spent away from home hurt Elvis's relationship with Priscilla too. The two rarely saw each other. Elvis was unhappy, both personally and professionally. He knew his life had to change.

On May 1, 1967, Elvis returned to Memphis for a joyful event. In a springtime ceremony, Elvis and Priscilla were married. Nine months later, on February 1, 1968, Lisa Marie Presley was born.

The birth of his daughter inspired Elvis to make a career move. He wanted to stay home with Priscilla and the new baby. He also longed to focus his creative energy on music. Elvis told the Colonel he would fulfill his last film contract, costarring with Mary Tyler Moore in *Change of Habit*. After that he would never act again.

Priscilla and Elvis are married.

In December 1968, Elvis reentered the music scene with an hour-long TV special. As the show opened, a blue neon sign flashed a simple message: "E-L-V-I-S." The band began to play. Then Elvis appeared, dressed in a tight, black leather suit. He sang one of his 1958 hits, "Trouble."

Elvis's career took off again in the late 1960s.

The music hit the audience like a bolt of lightning. They begged for more. Elvis sang many of his past hits such as "Can't Help Falling in Love" and "Guitar Man." He performed with power and enthusiasm. After years away from the music world, Elvis was back on top. "There is something magical about watching a man who has lost himself find his way back home," said one reviewer.

Elvis returned to RCA to make albums—the first music other than sound tracks he'd recorded in years. He worked with other studios too. At American Recording Studio in Memphis, Elvis taped "Suspicious Minds," "Long Black Limousine," and other songs that became hits.

In the summer of 1969, Elvis headed to the International Hotel in Las Vegas, Nevada, for a four-week concert engagement. Wearing rings and medallions, a caped jumpsuit studded with rhinestones, and thick "lamb-chop" sideburns, Elvis looked like a flashy Las Vegas showman. He performed two shows nightly, and the theater filled to capacity at every performance. His shows broke all attendance records in Las Vegas.

In 1971 the National Academy of Recording Arts and Sciences presented Elvis, only 36 years old, with its highest honor, the Lifetime Achievement Award. Elvis added the award to his growing collection of trophies, tributes, and gold and platinum records. Over time Elvis acquired 14 Grammy nominations from the academy and 3 Grammy awards.

Throughout the early 1970s, Elvis toured the United States. His concerts sold out wherever he went. People everywhere agreed—Elvis Presley was "the King of Rock and Roll."

But as Elvis continued to tour, his marriage suffered. He rarely saw Priscilla and little Lisa. Priscilla was lonely. In February 1972, she left Elvis for her karate teacher, Mike Stone, and filed for divorce. Elvis was heartbroken. "Her leaving him was, after his mother's death, probably the toughest single blow in his life," said a friend.

Elvis was happiest when he was in front of an audience.

For comfort, Elvis turned to music. In 1973 he performed a concert that most of the world could see. "Aloha from Hawaii" was broadcast live via satellite to 40 countries and 1.5 billion viewers. Never before had a musician performed to such a large audience. Elvis donated all the profits from the concert—nearly $85,000—to the Kui Lee Cancer Fund in Hawaii.

As his fame continued to grow, Elvis became weary. He had lost Priscilla, and the pressures of nonstop touring took their toll. Elvis saw a doctor about his fatigue. The doctor prescribed "uppers," drugs that would perk Elvis up before a concert, and "downers" to help him fall asleep at night. Soon Elvis began to abuse the medication. He became addicted to the drugs.

Elvis tried to kick his drug habit many times— without success. Meanwhile, his health began to deteriorate. Years of eating the fattening foods he loved—pork sausage, banana splits, biscuits, and his favorite, fried peanut butter-and-banana sandwiches—had caught up with him. By 1975 Elvis had put on more than 50 pounds. At first he was embarrassed to perform in public. His good looks had always been important to him. But soon Elvis realized that his fans accepted him at any size. He continued to tour.

Elvis's health took a troublesome turn in 1977. At age 42 he was so weak he could hardly sing. He sometimes forgot the words to songs while on-stage. Once, before a Louisville concert, he passed out. His friends and family advised him to cancel all upcoming shows and take a vacation.

"But the fans expect to see me," Elvis protested. "If it weren't for my fans, I wouldn't be where I am now. I owe everything to them."

One evening in August, Elvis played a game of racquetball with friends. Later, the group gathered around the piano at Graceland. Elvis was in a good mood and sang a few of his favorite songs. A few hours later, Elvis said good night to his friends and went to his room to read.

Sometime during the night, Elvis had a heart attack. In the morning, on Wednesday, August 16, 1977, Elvis was found dead.

Sadness spread across the nation as word of Elvis's death reached the American public. Most people couldn't believe the King was gone. More than 80,000 people jammed the street outside Graceland to pay respects to their hero. "Dozens swooned, cried, keened and passed out from the heat outside the mansion gates," reported *Time* magazine.

Grieving fans covered the lawn of Graceland with thousands of flowers. Large bouquets arrived in the shape of hound dogs and guitars. On the day Elvis Presley died, every florist in Memphis ran out of flowers.

6

The Legend Lives On

Fifteen years after his death, Elvis Presley reappeared. All over the United States, people lined up to buy the latest Elvis release. But the fans weren't after a record album. They wanted a 29-cent postage stamp!

On June 4, 1992, Priscilla Presley unveiled the "Elvis Stamp"—the U.S. Postal Service's tribute to Elvis Presley—during a ceremony at Graceland. Millions of Americans had voted on the design of the stamp, which showed Elvis as a handsome, young singing star of the 1950s.

At the ceremony, Priscilla—who had remained good friends with Elvis after their divorce—gave special thanks to Elvis's fans: "This would probably be the most special award to him," she said. "Elvis loved his fans very, very much, and I think he would have been just totally overwhelmed by your support."

The stamp went on sale in post offices across the nation on January 8, 1993—Elvis's birthday. In many locations, the stamp sold out immediately. The Postal Service expects the Elvis Stamp to be its biggest seller of all time.

The Elvis Stamp is just one of many ongoing tributes to Elvis Presley. With Priscilla's encouragement, Graceland was opened to the public in 1982. The mansion was placed on the National Register of Historic Places in 1991. Graceland is one of the most visited homes in America—second only to the White House.

Elvis's pink Cadillac is a favorite exhibit on the Graceland tour.

The pool room at Graceland

Touch Of Elvis

Oil

Elvis souvenirs are still popular, and impersonators like Elvis Herselvis keep Elvis's spirit alive.

At Graceland fans can see Elvis's home exactly as he left it in 1977. They can view Elvis's costumes, cars, and awards. His private jet, the *Lisa Marie*, is on display, as is the Meditation Garden, where Elvis, his parents, and Grandma Minnie Mae are buried. The garden also has a special memorial marker for Elvis's twin brother, Jesse Garon.

Lisa Marie Presley is the only heir to her father's fortune. She lives in the Los Angeles area with her husband and two children and is pursuing a singing career. Lisa is frequently featured in entertainment magazines—the public is always hungry for news about the Presley clan.

Every year Elvis gains new followers. Fans all over the world continue to buy his records and watch his movies. Thousands of Elvis impersonators perform nightly in clubs from Tokyo to Las Vegas. Elvis Presley fan clubs, more than 300 worldwide, still thrive, and collectors pay top dollar for Elvis photographs, autographs, and original recordings.

Some people claim they've recently seen Elvis—alive. One such "Elvis sighting" occurred in June 1988, when Louise Welling of Kalamazoo, Michigan, said she saw Elvis coming out of a local Burger King. Many people cannot accept the fact that the King is gone.

Indeed, years after his death, Elvis lives in the hearts of millions. What powerful force draws people to Elvis? "Elvis had a quality about him that I cannot describe," says one faithful fan. "I've never seen it in anyone else. He was *magic*."

ABOUT
THE AUTHOR

Katherine E. Krohn is the author of several books for young readers including *Lucille Ball: Pioneer of Comedy* and *Roseanne Arnold: Comedy's Queen Bee.* She lives in San Francisco.

ACKNOWLEDGMENTS

Photographs used with permission of Syndication International: pp. 1, 16, 49; © Elvis Presley Enterprises: pp. 2, 12, 22, 35 (bottom), 48, 52, 54, 59 (top and bottom), 62; Photofest: pp. 6, 9, 25, 37, 40, 47, 51; Hollywood Book and Poster: pp. 10, 32, 44, 56; UPI / Bettman, pp. 14, 21, 30, 39; Michael Ochs Archives: pp. 27, 29, 35 (top), 42, 63; U.S. Postal Service: p. 58; Independent Picture Service: p. 60 (top); Elvis Herselvis: p. 60 (bottom); Denise Slattery, p. 64. Front cover: Michael Ochs Archives; back cover: Photofest.